Discovering Cultures

Singapore

Dana Meachen Rau

BENCHMARK BOOKS

MARSHALL CAVENDISH
NEW YORK

With thanks to Minfong Ho, Cornell University, for the careful review of this manuscript.

Marshall Cavendish
99 White Plains Road
Tarrytown, New York 10591-9001
www.marshallcavendish.com

All Internet sites were available and accurate when sent to press.

Library of Congress Cataloging-in-Publication Data

Rau, Dana Meachen, 1971–
Singapore / by Dana Meachen Rau.
p. cm. — (Discovering cultures)
Summary: An introduction to the geography, history, people, and culture of Singapore.
Includes bibliographical references and index.
ISBN 0-7614-1727-3
1. Singapore —Juvenile literature. [1. Singapore.] I. Title. II. Series.
DS609.R38 2003
959.57—dc22   2003019102

Photo Research by Candlepants Incorporated

Cover Photo: Kevin R. Morris /Corbis

The photographs in this book are used by permission and through the courtesy of; *Corbis*: James Marshall, 1; Michael S. Yamashita, 4, 12, 42 (lower); Paul Russell, 6-7; Kevin R. Morris, 8, 18, 30; Robert Holmes, 9, 19 (lower); Jack Hollingsworth, 10, 24, 42 (lower left), back cover; Michael Garrett, 13; Bob Krist, 16; Wolfgang Kaehler, 23; Carl & Ann Purcell, 26, 37; Paul Russell, 27, 42 (center); Kevin Christopher/OU Photography, 28; AFP, 29; Dean Conger, 34-35; Morton Beebe, 38; Marcus Oleniuk, 45; *Robert Fried*: 11 (both), 31; 43 (top). *The Image Works*: James Marshall. 17, 43 (lower right); Bill Bachmann, 22; Topham, 32; Hideo Haga/HAGA, 33; HAGA, 36; *Getty Images*: Alan Becker, 14; *Envision*: Steven Needham, 19 (top); *Joyce Photographics/PhotoResearchers Inc.*: 20.

Cover: *Large sculpture of a merlion, the symbol of Singapore*; Title page: *Hindu girl dressed for a festival*

Map and illustrations by Ian Warpole
Book design by Virginia Pope

Printed in China
1 3 5 6 4 2

Turn the Pages...

Where in the World Is Singapore?

Each day, the steamy sun rises over Singapore. Singapore is a country in Southeast Asia. It includes one small main island, surrounded by about sixty even smaller islands. The main island of Singapore is smaller than any of the fifty United States. From east to west, it stretches about 25 miles (42 kilometers). North to south, it is only 14 miles (23 km).

Singapore's closest neighbors are Malaysia in the north and Indonesia to the south and east. It lies in a spot where the South China Sea meets the Indian Ocean. Singapore is separated from Malaysia by a

A trap for fish along the coast of Singapore

4

Map of Singapore

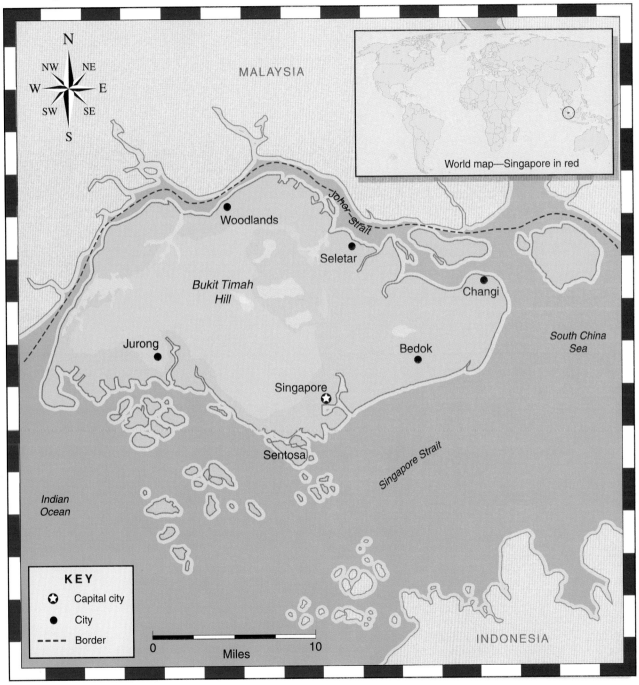

MALAYSIA

N
NW · NE
W · E
SW · SE
S

World map—Singapore in red

Johor Strait

Woodlands

Seletar

Bukit Timah
Hill

Changi

Jurong

Bedok

South China
Sea

Singapore

Sentosa

Singapore Strait

Indian
Ocean

INDONESIA

KEY

⬡ Capital city

● City

- - - - Border

0   Miles   10

5

thin strip of water called the Johor Strait. It is separated from Indonesia by the Singapore Strait.

Hot and rainy best describe Singapore's weather. The climate is tropical. That means the temperature is hot and the air is very wet. Singapore's temperature is usually about 80 degrees Fahrenheit (27 degrees Celsius). Every year, about 95 inches (230 centimeters) of rain falls. Two *monsoons* blow across the country during the year. From December to March, the northeast monsoon blows. The southwestern monsoon blows from June to September. In between the monsoons, thunderstorms pass through the country.

The land of Singapore is hilly in the west and center, and flat in the east. There is not much farming. Most business is done in the city of Singapore.

The city of Singapore is the country's capital. It shares the same name as the

Tall buildings make up the skyline of the city of Singapore.

Ships from around the world stop in Singapore's port.

country itself. The city of Singapore is important worldwide. Singapore has the largest *port* in Southeast Asia, and one of the largest ports in the world. Ships are constantly coming and going. Singapore trades products with countries such as Malaysia, Indonesia, the United States, and Japan. It ships out machinery and electronic equipment, as well as smaller items, such as tropical fish. Foreign ships also bring products, such as iron, steel, fuel, and food, to Singapore to sell. Many countries use the port of Singapore as a stopover on their way to trade with other countries.

Bukit Timah Nature Reserve

Long ago, Sang Nila Utama, a Sumatran prince, sailed to the island named Temasek, which means Sea Town. While there, he hunted wild animals in the thick tropical rain forests that covered the land. He believed he saw a lion there. He decided to start a city on the island, and to call it "Singa Pura," which means Lion City.

Lions probably did not live in the rain forests that once covered Singapore. But they were filled with tigers, wild boars, and other large animals. When settlers cut down the forests, these animals died out.

Now, only a small piece of rain forest remains in the Bukit Timah Nature Reserve. The *reserve* also includes Singapore's highest point—Bukit Timah Hill—which rises 538 feet (164 meters). Trails wind through the forest. Huge trees tower overhead. Many kinds of ferns cover the ground below. One might spot tree shrews, flying lemurs, insects, birds, pythons, lizards, and more in the rain for- est. Friendly and playful long-tailed macaques live here and also like to greet visitors.

What Makes Singapore Singaporean?

Singapore is filled with groups of people who have very different backgrounds and beliefs. About four million people live in Singapore. Most of them, about 77 percent, are Chinese. Malay citizens make up about 14 percent of the population, and people from India make up about 8 percent. The rest are from other countries around the globe. Because

Singaporeans spending an afternoon in the park

of its many different people, Singapore has four official languages—Chinese, Malay, Tamil (Indian), and English. English is the language most used in business. The national language of Singapore is Malay.

Several religions are followed in Singapore. Most of the Chinese are Buddhists or Taoists. The Malays are Muslims, and most Indians are Hindus. Some people are Christians. Many places of worship—temples, mosques, and churches—can be found throughout the country.

A Buddhist statue

A Hindu man prays in a temple.

How do such different people live together? Singaporeans live, shop, and work with each other every day. They share their foods and traditions with each other. The government has made sure that their communities work together.

The head of Singapore's government is the president. The people vote for the president in an election. A prime minister runs the government. The prime minister is usually the leader of the political party that received the most votes in the election. A parliament is also elected to make the laws for the country.

The people of Singapore live in a modern world. They keep up with the latest trends and styles. Most Singaporeans dress the way people do in the United States. However, some

Malay women still wear a long-sleeved shirt called a *baju kurung* and a long skirt called a *sarung*. Traditional dress is often saved for special occasions—such as the long, colorful sari that Indian women wrap around their bodies. During the holidays, Chinese women may wear a *cheongsam*, a traditional Chinese dress.

Most Singaporeans work hard—Monday through Friday, and half-days on Saturday. They want to be successful at what they do. Most people work in the

A Malay Muslim woman wearing a traditional head covering

city. Many work in banking and business offices. Some work in stores or in hotels and restaurants. Other people work in factories.

Outside the city, there is some farming. About 1 percent of the population are farmers. The farms of Singapore are bursting with color. There are farms that grow fruits called *durians*, *mangosteens*, and *rambutans*. Orchids, a type of flower, are also grown, mostly to be sold to other countries. Fish farms raise colorful aquarium fish.

Baskets for sale on a city street

The arts are very important in Singapore. The Singapore Art Museum displays art from artists worldwide, as well as many works by Singaporeans. Many traditional arts and crafts, such as Chinese *calligraphy*, Malay baskets, and beautiful Indian flower *garlands*, can still be seen as you walk through the city. *Operas* are also very popular. Wayang performances are Chinese operas. The opera stories come from Chinese history or folklore. The actors wear very detailed costumes and makeup.

A traditional Chinese wayang performance

The Singapore Symphony Orchestra brings classical and modern music to Singapore. They play at the Victoria Concert Hall or in outdoor concerts.

Dancing is enjoyed by many Singaporeans. The Singapore Dance Theater performs ballet and modern dances for large crowds. There are also traditional dances. Young Indian girls may learn the Bharatanatyam. In a Malay dance called the Kuda Kepang men reenact battle scenes on wooden horses and then walk across glass to the tune of Malay music.

Feng Shui

Feng shui is a traditional Chinese belief. It is based on the idea that people should live in harmony with the world around them. In Chinese, the word *feng* means "wind" and *shui* means "water." In feng shui, the way a building is placed in the landscape, or the way furniture is placed in a room, can affect how lucky, wealthy, or healthy someone will be. People who practice feng shui believe *chi* (energy) is constantly flowing around them. Good chi must be able to flow easily around a space, and not be trapped in a corner. People throughout Singapore use the idea of feng shui when designing homes and office buildings.

Living in Singapore

Long ago, most Singaporeans lived near the *harbor*. As people from other countries came to live in Singapore, the area around the harbor became crowded. A city plan created in the 1800s divided the people into separate neighborhoods, or *kampongs*. Where people lived depended on where they came from. There was a Chinese neighborhood, a Malay neighborhood, and an Indian neighborhood.

Homes near the center of the city

A crowded street in Chinatown

As even more people came to live in Singapore, the city became crowded and dirty. In 1960, the government created the Housing and Development Board (HDB). The HDB built homes that the people could afford outside the city. Housing estates are groups of tall high-rise apartment buildings. Each estate has its own schools, stores, doctors, playgrounds, gyms, and movie theaters.

Today, more than three-quarters of Singaporeans live in housing estates. Other people live in private homes or in apartments inside the city itself. The original neighborhoods still exist. They are called Chinatown, Little India, and Kampong Glam (the Malay district).

Singapore is filled with tall buildings, highways, and public housing. But planners try their best to be sure there are beautiful parks filled with trees and flowers throughout the island and the city itself. Singapore is sometimes even called the Garden City.

The city of Singapore is a clean and safe place compared to many other cities of the world. Part of this is because it has very strict laws. Acts as simple as spitting in public or crossing in the middle of a street have very strict punishments.

In Singapore, people often greet each other by asking, "Ni chi bao le ma?" That means "Have you eaten yet?" Sharing meals is an important part of Singaporean life.

The fact that people in Singapore came from China, Malaysia, and India is reflected in their foods. The flavors of the foods from all the groups have mixed. But each culture still has its own traditional foods. Most Chinese meals start with rice. With it comes pork, chicken, duck, or fish. Soup is popular, as well as different kinds of green vegetables. Many of their dishes are spicy

Beautiful flowers, such as these orchids, can be found in gardens throughout Singapore.

and hot. Usually, a Chinese meal is eaten with a group who share dishes in the center of the table. A popular lunch is *dim sum*. Dim sum are dumplings filled with meat and vegetables. Between meals, noodles are a popular snack. Tea is the most popular drink.

The food of the Malay people is also based on rice. The Malays eat a lot of chicken and fish but no pork, because they are Muslims. They

Some of the foods served during a dim sum lunch

Friends share a meal.

Singaporeans often eat fruit for dessert, such as this durian.

add the flavors of hot chilies and coconut milk. *Satay* is a popular Malay dish. Satay is made with pieces of meat barbequed on metal sticks called skewers. It is dipped in a peanut sauce.

Many Indians practice Hinduism and are vegetarians. That means they do not eat meat. Instead, they eat a variety of beans, such as chickpeas or lentils.

Desserts are often simple. Fruit is popular, such as papayas, mangosteens, and durians. Kueh desserts make delicious after-dinner treats. They are small, colorful cakes made with coconut.

Let's Eat!
Kaya

Kaya is a sweet jam made of eggs, sugar, and coconut that Singaporeans often spread on bread and eat for breakfast. Ask an adult to help you prepare this recipe.

Ingredients:

1 cup white sugar

5 eggs

7 ounces canned coconut milk

Wash your hands. In a bowl, crack the five eggs. Beat with a mixer on medium speed. Add the sugar and mix on high. Add the coconut milk and continue mixing until all the sugar is dissolved. Boil water in the bottom pan of a double boiler. Pour the mixture into the top pan. Stir constantly and scrape the bottom of the pan or the kaya will stick and burn. The kaya will get thicker. It will also turn color from yellowish white to reddish brown. This may take up to forty-five minutes. When it has all changed color, take the pan off the heat and cool. Spread the kaya on bread. It is a sweet and delicious way to start the day!

School Days

Education is very important to the people of Singapore. All children are expected to study hard. If they are successful students, then it is likely that they will become successful members of Singapore's workforce as adults.

For a long time in Singapore, children did not have to go to school. In the 1900s, the government decided to make education more important. Today, all children must go to school. The government puts a lot of money into keeping its schools the best. About 94 percent of Singaporeans can read and write.

Children start primary school at age six. Some start a year or two earlier at preschool or kindergarten. Primary school lasts six years. Children learn math, science, and social studies. They also attend arts and crafts, physical education, and music classes. In many schools, the day is divided into two sessions so that all children have a chance to go. The morning session

A group of primary school students ready for class

lasts from 7:00 A.M. to 12:00 P.M. The afternoon session lasts from 1:00 P.M. to 6:00 P.M. Children attend one session or the other.

Language is an important subject in school. Starting in primary school and throughout their education, all students learn English. They also learn another one of the official languages of Singapore—Chinese, Malay, or Tamil—depending on their family's culture.

Most students take a bus to school. School lasts Monday through Friday, and then a half-day on Saturdays. Parents pay for a child's books and uniforms. The school sells lunches and snacks. After school, children might go to dance classes, music lessons, or school clubs.

After primary school, all students take an exam before they go on to secondary school, or high school. In secondary school, some students

Students take a field trip to the park.

take classes that focus on math and science. Others take classes focusing on the arts, including English, history, and geography. When they have completed four years of secondary school, some students leave to attend schools that teach job skills. Many students stay in secondary school for five years and then enter a junior college. There they spend two or three years preparing to study in a university. After completing junior college, students may attend universities both in and out of the country. Many students go to the National University of Singapore.

High school students study hard for a test.

Moral Education

In Singaporean schools, students receive moral education. These are lessons that teach them how to choose between what is right and what is wrong. Students learn to be proud of their country. They learn about the importance of family. They learn to help each other and the community. Instead of arguing, they learn ways to get along with others. Even though people in Singapore are from different backgrounds and religions, children learn to respect all people.

Just for Fun

Shopping malls are fun places to spend money and free time.

Singaporeans enjoy their free time. On Saturdays, when school and work are done for the day, shoppers fill the city streets. Teenagers gather at malls to meet friends and to eat.

Restaurants serve all types of food. But for a quick bite, Singaporeans visit hawker centers. Long ago, hawker centers were made up of moveable carts. Today, the sites are permanent. Food stalls line each side, and tables fill the center. Hungry customers check the boards to see what is on the menu. They order drinks from one stall, noodles from another, and dessert from a third. The food is brought to their tables. Hawker centers are a

Singaporeans enjoy an evening out.

quick way to get inexpensive Chinese, Malay, and Indian food in the middle of the busy city.

Like people in the United States, Singaporeans spend a lot of their free time watching television, listening to music, surfing the Internet, or going to

Swimming in a local pool

the movies. However, the government keeps tight control on what can be seen and heard.

Singapore's top three sports are jogging, swimming, and walking. The sports complexes in each housing estate usually have swimming pools. The many parks across the country are connected with paths for jogging and walking.

Women's soccer draws many fans to its exciting games.

Singaporeans love to watch soccer and horse racing. They also play cricket, water sports, and track and field. They ride skateboards and bicycles. Some Singaporeans practice tai chi. This is a type of martial art with slow movements that are meant to relax one's mind, while making the body strong.

For fun, some people get together to play the traditional Chinese game of mah-jongg. It is played with tiles engraved with Chinese characters.

When Singaporeans want to get away for the day, they can easily travel around the island on the train. The train connects the city with the rest of the country. Getting from one end of the country to the other takes only about an hour.

The island of Sentosa is connected to Singapore by a beautiful bridge.

Singapore is filled with parks that people love to visit, such as the Chinese and Japanese gardens. Malaysia is so close that people can also go there for the day by driving over a bridge that connects the two countries. The smaller islands of Singapore are also nice to visit. Sentosa, one of Singapore's islands, is a popular place for vacations.

Singing Contests

Songbirds are popular pets in Singapore. The cages that hold these tiny creatures are sometimes very detailed and beautiful. On Sunday mornings, some people bring their cages and birds to neighborhood parks and hang them up on poles. People enjoy listening to the birds sing. Sometimes, they hold contests to see whose bird sings the best.

Let's Celebrate!

Singapore has many national holidays. Chinese New Year occurs in January or February. It marks the start of a new year on the Chinese calendar. Each year is named after a different animal—the ox, tiger, dragon, snake, and others. On the night before the new year begins, families join together for a traditional meal called the family reunion dinner. The holiday lasts fifteen days. On the first two days of the holiday, schools and businesses are closed.

Chingay parades are filled with music, dancing, and dragons!

During new year celebrations, houses are decorated with red and gold colors. Chinatown, especially, is filled with decorations and lights. Some people decorate with kumquat trees. They are a symbol of good luck. Parents and relatives give their children red envelopes called *hong baos*. They are filled with lucky coins. Chinese New Year ends with the Chingay Procession—a huge parade of decorated floats, dancers, and bands.

In the middle of autumn, when the moon is bright, Singaporeans celebrate the Mooncake Festival or Lantern Festival. At this time, children parade through the streets carrying paper lanterns. All over Singapore, people eat mooncakes. Mooncakes are molded round cakes filled with black

A Chingay dancer in a colorful costume

beans or sweet fillings. Messages decorate the tops of mooncakes. An ancient legend says that mooncakes were once marked with secret messages. They were used to spread news about a revolt against a cruel emperor.

One of the most important Muslim holidays is Hari Raya Puasa. This day marks the end of the month of Ramadan. Ramadan is a holy time of prayer and fasting. Muslims fast from sunrise to sunset. This means they do not eat during the day. On Hari Raya Puasa, families visit mosques and pray. Then they join their families and friends for a feast.

Beautiful paper lanterns on display during the Lantern Festival

Bright lights shine in the dark during Deepavali.

Hindus celebrate Deepavali in October. Deepavali is a festival of lights. Lamps and lights decorate streets and homes. This holiday celebrates the power of good over evil and light over darkness. Deepavali is a time to dress in new clothes, pray at temples, and eat together.

Christmas decorations in Singapore

Easter and Christmas are also celebrated in Singapore. The traditions for these holidays are much the same as they are in the United States. Children eat chocolate eggs on Easter. On Christmas, people give gifts and decorate with lights and trees.

The parade on National Day is fun for everyone.

Everyone in Singapore celebrates National Day on August 9. This marks the day that Singapore became an independent nation in 1965. Before then, it had been a part of Malaysia. People celebrate all month long. On National Day, there is a huge parade. The parade usually ends in the National Stadium in front of a large crowd. In the evening there is a party in the streets. It is a time for the country to celebrate Singapore together.

The Dragon Boat Festival

The Dragon Boat Festival is an event held each year in late May or June. It honors the popular poet Qu Yuan, who drowned himself almost 2,500 years ago in China's Mei Lo River. Teams from Singapore and around the world come together at East Coast Park to compete in an exciting race. The race symbolizes the rowing of the fishermen who hurried to save Qu Yuan. Long boats are filled with as many as twenty-four rowers. They row to the rhythm of drums. Their boats are brightly painted with scales, tails, and heads to look like dragons.

Singapore's flag has a band of red and a band of white. The red stands for the equality of all people. White stands for purity. In the top left corner is a crescent moon with five stars. The crescent moon means that Singapore is a young country growing larger. The stars stand for progress, democracy, peace, equality, and justice.

The money of Singapore is called the Singapore dollar. In 2003, about 1.74 Singapore dollars equaled one U.S. dollar.

Count in Malay

English	Malay	Say it like this:
one	satu	SA-too
two	dua	DOO-a
three	tiga	TIE-ga
four	empat	EM-pat
five	lima	LEE-ma
six	enam	EN-am
seven	tujuh	TOO-juh
eight	lapan	LAP-an
nine	sembilan	SEM-bil-an
ten	sepuluh	SE-pull-uh

Glossary

calligraphy   A traditional form of decorative writing.

durian   A tasty, large fruit with a strong smell and a prickly skin.

garland   A necklace made of fresh flowers.

harbor   A sheltered place along a coast where ships can anchor.

mangosteen   A juicy, thick-skinned fruit that tastes like both a peach and a pineapple.

monsoon   A strong wind that blows at specific times every year.

opera   A musical production that tells a story.

port   A place on the shore where ships drop off or pick up cargo.

rambutan   A bright red fruit with a prickly skin.

reserve   A protected place where animals can live safely.

Fast Facts

The main island of Singapore is smaller than any of the fifty United States. From east to west, it stretches about 25 miles (42 km). North to south, it is only 14 miles (23 km).

Singapore is a country in Southeast Asia. It includes one small main island, surrounded by about sixty even smaller islands.

Singapore's highest point is Bukit Timah Hill, which rises 538 feet (164 m).

The city of Singapore is the country's capital. It shares the same name as the country itself.

Singapore's flag has a band of red and a band of white. The red stands for equality and the white stands for purity. The crescent moon means that Singapore is a young country growing larger. The stars stand for progress, democracy, peace, equality, and justice.

Singapore's climate is tropical. The temperature is usually about 80 degrees Fahrenheit (27 degrees C). Every year, about 95 inches (230 cm) of rain falls.

42

Several religions are
followed in Singapore. Most of the
Chinese are Buddhists or Taoists. The Malays
are Muslims, and most Indians are Hindus.
Some people are Christians.

The money of
Singapore is called
the Singapore dollar.
In 2003, about 1.74
Singapore dollars
equaled one
U.S. dollar.

The head of Singapore's government is the
president. A prime minister runs the government. A parliament
makes the laws for the country.

As of July 2003, there were
4,608,595 people living in Singapore.
About 77 percent were Chinese, 14 percent
were Malay, and 8 percent were Indian. The
rest were from other countries.

Singapore
has four
official
languages—
Chinese, Malay,
Tamil (Indian), and
English. English is the language most
used in business. The national
language of Singapore
is Malay.

Proud to Be Singaporean

Catherine Lim (1942–)

Catherine Lim is a famous Singaporean author. She was born and raised in Malaysia and lives in Singapore. Lim's collections of short stories and novels have been published and read by people around the world. She often writes about women's issues. She is also known for her speeches about Chinese culture and women's rights.

Sir Thomas Stamford Raffles (1781–1826)

Sir Thomas Stamford Raffles first came to Singapore in 1819. He worked for the British East India Company. He came to Singapore because he thought it would be a good place to set up a trading post. He was right. Many people came to Singapore to do business and to live. Chinese, Malays, and especially Indians settled in the region. Raffles came up with a town plan to create neighborhoods for all the new people. He was responsible for making Singapore the largest port in Southeast Asia and a land of diverse people and ideas.

Lee Kuan Yew (1923–)

Lee Kuan Yew was born and raised in Singapore with his Chinese family. He studied law in Britain, then returned to Singapore and became involved in government. Lee Kuan Yew served as Singapore's first prime minister from 1959 to 1990. He turned Singapore into an independent, successful, and wealthy country. He also helped the people to get along. Today, Lee Kuan Yew is still involved in Singapore's government as the senior minister.

Find Out More

Books

Chinese Festivals Cookbook by Stuart Thompson, Angela Dennington, and Zul Mukhida. Raintree-Steck/Vaughn, Austin, Texas, 2001.

Countries of the World: Singapore by James Michael Baker and Junia Marion Baker. Gareth Stevens Publishing, Milwaukee, Wisconsin, 2002.

Moonbeams, Dumplings and Dragon Boats by Nina Simonds and Leslie Swartz. Gulliver Books, San Diego, California, 2002.

Singapore by Matt Thomas. The Child's World, Chanhassen, Minnesota, 2002.

Web Sites*

http://www.nparks.gov.sg/
The National Parks Board of Singapore describes all of Singapore's national parks and lists upcoming events and information about visiting these beautiful places.

http://www.sg/kids/
Singapore's Infomap for Kids is Singapore's national Web site with all types of information about Singapore, including its geography, people, national symbols, and amazing facts.

http://www.odci.gov/cia/publications/factbook/geos/sn.html
The World Factbook lists all the important facts about Singapore, with information about the land, people, government, and business.

*All Internet sites were available and accurate when sent to press.

Index

Page numbers for illustrations are in **boldface.**

About the Author

Dana Meachen Rau is an author, editor, and illustrator. A graduate of Trinity College in Hartford, Connecticut, she has written almost one hundred books for children, including nonfiction, biographies, early readers, and historical fiction. Ms. Rau is happiest sipping a cup of hot cocoa on her blue sofa writing with her pad and pen. She lives and works in Burlington, Connecticut, with her husband, Chris, and children, Charlie and Allison.